Logging and Monitoring Challenges with AWS Fargate

Table of Contents

Chapter 1. Introduction

In this Special Report, we delve into the topic of 'Logging and Monitoring Challenges with AWS Fargate', a subject that holds significant gravity in the realms of cloud computing. This doesn't appear to be your typical easygoing read-it-during-lunchtime report; instead, it's a deeply technical dive that spans across important concepts and practical complexities related to container management using AWS Fargate. We aim to prepare you to deftly handle the challenges and intricacies associated with logging and monitoring in this AWS service. If you're striving to optimize your system's performance or troubleshooting efforts, this report is an invaluable resource. So, strap on your problem-solving hats, and let's navigate the intricate labyrinth of AWS Fargate together.

Chapter 2. Introduction to AWS Fargate and Its Importance

AWS Fargate is a serverless compute engine provided by Amazon Web Services (AWS) for containers. Fargate allows developers to focus on designing and building their applications, free of the administrative burden of managing the infrastructure underlying the application execution area.

Fargate facilitates easy scalability and its efficient design model contributes to optimal resource utilization, thereby enhancing the performance of systems deployed on the cloud. With Fargate, you can run containers without having to manage servers or clusters. This service automatically manages the scaling and administration of your infrastructure, allowing you to focus more on developing your applications.

2.1. Containerization and AWS Fargate

Containerization is a system-wide hierarchical technology that involves encapsulating an application in a container with its own operating environment. This method of software management has numerous advantages including code portability, simplified scaling, and application isolation, which eradicates the issue of conflicting software dependencies.

Containers are designed for a fast-paced, continuous integration and continuous delivery (CI/CD) life cycle. AWS Fargate was developed in response to these fast-evolving trends in software development and deployment, providing a reliable and efficient method to run containers at scale.

What sets Fargate apart is the ease with which it manages containers, as it simplifies deployment and scalability while minimizing the need for manual intervention. In the context of AWS, Fargate natively integrates with most AWS services such as Elastic Load Balancer (ELB), Amazon RDS, and Amazon S3. It also enables you to follow the same IAM roles and policies that you may already be using for your other AWS services thus tightly integrating into your AWS ecosystem.

2.2. Importance of AWS Fargate

The agility, scalability, and speed offered by AWS Fargate make it a vital tool for businesses striving for efficiency in a cloud-native environment. Its relevance in today's digitized world is highlighted by its multiple advantages:

1. **Facilitated Operations**: One of the biggest advantages offered by AWS Fargate is its automated operational management. There's no need to spin up, update, or monitor underlying servers resulting in streamlined and automated infrastructure operations.

2. **Resource Optimization**: AWS Fargate allows for precise resource specification. You can define your CPU and memory configuration, and pay only for what you use. This facility helps optimize the allocation of resources, consequently increasing the efficiency of your operations.

3. **Enhanced Security**: AWS Fargate ensures high levels of isolation between containers, reducing risk. Your application is further protected as Fargate derives task-level IAM roles and security groups.

4. **Scalability**: With AWS Fargate, scaling is easy and efficient. It effortlessly handles changes in demand, making it an ideal choice for variable workloads.

5. **Integration**: Fargate integrates seamlessly with other AWS services. For example, AWS CloudTrail captures a record of each Fargate API event, while AWS CloudWatch can be used to view operational metrics.

2.3. AWS Fargate in real-world scenarios

In a business where a large-scale website needs to rapidly scale out due to sudden high traffic, traditional methods can cause manual effort, time consumption, and delayed response. AWS Fargate can help remedy this situation by auto-scaling in response to traffic conditions, ensuring smooth operations.

Another instance would be in the deployment of microservices, where managing each service's infrastructure is a challenge. AWS Fargate could enable the use of containers to separate each microservice without the need to manage individual servers or clusters, thus simplifying the container management.

However, considering the immense complexity and impact of AWS Fargate, its practical implementation requires a keen understanding of some associated complexities, particularly the challenges with logging and monitoring. In the subsequent sections of this report, we will explore these in greater depth, trying to provide a relieving solution to each complexity.

It's important to note that adopting AWS Fargate does not absolve the responsibility of monitoring your applications and infrastructure. Rather, Fargate makes monitoring more important because you must configure scaling and availability policies, and track the performance of your applications to ensure they are operating efficiently.

This report will cover the array of challenges you may encounter and provide clarity on the solutions possible when dealing with logging and monitoring in AWS Fargate.

Chapter 3. Understanding AWS Fargate Logging Fundamentals

Logging is an imperative process in cloud computing and application management. As simple as it may seem to monitor or log services, every technology brings its associated complications. AWS Fargate, in all its glory and convenience, also comes with its unique logging challenges. To understand these challenges and solve these, we delve first into the fundamentals of logging with AWS Fargate.

3.1. What is Logging in AWS Fargate?

Before plunging into the techniques, pitfalls, and best practices, we need to set a firm foundation - understanding what we mean by logging in AWS Fargate. Logging captures and stores information about the events happening within your application. This could include data about incoming requests, system errors, system health, security-related activities, or even user behavior. Each recorded event, known as a log entry, is timestamped and usually contains other auxiliary information.

In the context of Fargate, logs can help track the performance and health of your containers, troubleshoot any issues that arise, and monitor usage patterns or potential security risks implicit in your service.

3.2. Choosing a Logging Solution for AWS Fargate

When deciding on a logging solution, you are mainly looking for a way to effectively collect, store, and analyze log data. AWS provides several native solutions, but third-party logging services like Loggly or Kibana are also viable options. Your choice of logging solution will depend on factors like your specific log data requirements, your budget, and the overall complexity of your cloud environment.

Let's take a moment to introduce one of the most common native logging solutions provided by AWS: CloudWatch Logs. AWS CloudWatch Logs allows you to monitor, store, and access your log files from AWS resources. It provides a robust feature of automatically sending log files from your applications to CloudWatch Logs and to monitor, in real-time, the logs for specific phrases, values, or patterns.

3.3. Logging Mechanisms in AWS Fargate

There are two mechanisms by which you can implement logs in AWS Fargate: the awslogs log driver and the FireLens log router. Here's what you need to know about each.

1. AWSLogs Log Driver: The awslogs driver allows you to directly log your events from within your service to CloudWatch Logs. If you are using this log driver, you need to ensure your task execution IAM role has the necessary CloudWatch permissions.

2. FireLens Log Router: FireLens is a recent addition to Fargate's logging capabilities. This tool serves as a log router built on Fluent Bit, which allows you to route logs to an extensive array of destinations, well beyond CloudWatch alone.

3.4. How To Enable Logging in AWS Fargate?

To activate logging for your Fargate tasks, you must specify it within your task definition at setup. Here is a quick walkthrough:

1. In the AWS Management Console, select 'ECS' under the 'Services' tab.

2. Then, choose 'Task Definitions' and create a new one by hitting 'Create new Task Definition.'

3. Walkthrough the creation wizard and under the container definition, scroll to the 'Storage and Logging' section.

4. Here, you can enable/disable auto-configuration for CloudWatch Logs. If enabled, logs will be automatically streamed to a new log group in CloudWatch.

3.5. Privacy and Security Considerations

While logging is a vital part of monitoring and debugging, remember that not all information should be logged due to privacy and security constraints. It's crucial to avoid logging sensitive data such as usernames, passwords or credit card details directly into log files.

In AWS Fargate, it's recommended to apply key management and encryption practices to log data, use Identity and Access Management (IAM) to ensure only those with appropriate access can access log data and consider employing Virtual Private Cloud (VPC) flow logs to capture information about the IP traffic flowing to your workloads.

To tackle the complex world of logging in AWS Fargate, it's best to start with a solid understanding of the fundamentals. AWS Fargate provides you numerous options for traffic filtration, encapsulation, and even automatic task alignment with the right setup. Being aware of the storage and handling of your logs can be a game-changer when it comes to troubleshooting and optimizing your system's performance in the AWS ecosystem.

Chapter 4. Deep Dive into AWS Fargate Monitoring Techniques

Logging and monitoring services are indispensable components of effective container management. In a vastly scalable environment such as provided by AWS Fargate, these services take on even more importance. AWS Fargate manages orchestration, removing the need to maintain a layered, ongoing infrastructure, but this gives rise to its own challenges. This chapter dives deep into the ins and outs of monitoring techniques with AWS Fargate.

4.1. Understanding AWS Fargate Monitoring

AWS Fargate, being a serverless compute engine for containers, allows users to focus on deploying applications without needing to manage an underlying infrastructure. Despite this simplification, monitoring the performance of these applications remains a vital aspect to ensure their optimal operation. AWS provides several tools to make this task more efficient, such as AWS CloudWatch, AWS X-Ray, and custom metrics.

Let's start with AWS CloudWatch. CloudWatch collects logging and monitoring data in form of logs, metrics, and events. But how does this work with Fargate? Well, Fargate tasks and services send metrics to CloudWatch every minute, providing you with real-time insight into resource utilization within your containerized applications.

AWS X-Ray complements CloudWatch by providing insights about connections between services, latency bottlenecks, and troubleshooting performance. X-Ray collects data about requests that your application serves and provides tools for understanding how services are interrelated and aiding in detecting where high latencies are occurring.

Moreover, custom metrics can be published to CloudWatch, which provides additional flexibility where standard metrics aren't sufficient. They prove to be invaluable when needing to monitor unique business requirements or application specific KPIs.

4.2. AWS CloudWatch and AWS Fargate: An Indispensable Pair

Containers managed by Fargate are ephemeral and non-persistent. Since Fargate handles the orchestration automatically, conventional techniques of logging which involve logging into the host running the container aren't feasible. AWS CloudWatch becomes invaluable here.

Fargate tasks send container-level CPU and memory utilization metrics to CloudWatch. This means that you can monitor your containers based on the percent CPU units used and the percent of memory utilized.

Succeeding with CloudWatch involves understanding and interpreting these logs and metrics. Events like throttling, error rates, latency, and more can be sorted and filtered with specified date and time ranges.

4.3. Deep Dive into AWS X-Ray

With AWS X-Ray, we can get more granular insights. It allows you to visualize, monitor, and troubleshoot the performance of your applications and their underlying services.

X-Ray provides an end-to-end view of requests as they travel through your application, showing a map of your application's underlying components. You can use X-Ray to analyze both applications in development and in production, from distributed applications to complex microservices.

Integrating X-Ray with AWS Fargate involves including X-Ray daemon sidecar in your task definition. Remember, X-Ray daemon must have permissions to upload trace data to the X-Ray service, hence IAM roles play a crucial part in the arrangement.

4.4. Custom Metrics: Adding Flexibility to Fargate Monitoring

AWS Fargate allows the publishing of custom metrics to CloudWatch. As stated before, not all monitoring requirements can be met with the provided metrics, therefore having a possibility to introduce custom metrics is a game changer. They allow you to define and monitor metrics that are unique to your application, infrastructure or business needs.

Setting up custom metrics requires you to include CloudWatch agent in your task definition. This agent is capable of monitoring host-level metrics beyond the default ones provided by Fargate and pushing them to CloudWatch.

4.5. Overcoming Fargate Logging and Monitoring Challenges

Though AWS Fargate offers many tools to simplify logging and monitoring, some challenges persist. For example, lacking access to the underlying infrastructure can make troubleshooting more complex. In such cases, the detailed metrics and logs provided by CloudWatch and X-Ray become incredibly vital.

Moreover, understanding how to best structure and interpret the vast amount of monitoring data can also prove daunting. Here, adopting a methodological approach towards monitoring and leveraging the power of setting custom metrics, alarms and utilizing CloudWatch dashboards can greatly enhance your troubleshooting efforts.

In conclusion, AWS Fargate, with its serverless architecture, presents both opportunities and challenges when it comes to monitoring. It's indispensable to understand the capabilities and constraints of tools like AWS CloudWatch, AWS X-Ray, and custom metrics. By harnessing these tools effectively, and understanding their role in monitoring the functioning of your applications, you can successfully navigate the intricate world of AWS Fargate monitoring.

Chapter 5. Challenges faced with AWS Fargate Logging and Monitoring

In the world of AWS's serverless compute engine, Fargate, logging and monitoring pose certain challenges that demand efficient and effective troubleshooting skills. To understand these fully, we will first delve into the main facets of Fargate and then head onto the specific impediments associated with logging and monitoring.

5.1. AWS Fargate: A Brief Overview

Created by Amazon Web Services (AWS), Fargate is a serverless compute engine designed for containers. This revolutionary service eliminates the need for server configuration, thereby simplifying the process of running containers. Despite its many advantages, like other services, Fargate is not without its challenges, particularly concerning its logging and monitoring.

5.2. Understanding Logging in AWS Fargate

Within AWS Fargate, logging is more intricate than traditional applications. Implementing effective logging strategies often requires detailed understanding of the available logging drivers and their configurations, coupled with a clear insight into the service's architecture. A robust Fargate logging system will typically publish logs via drivers directly to AWS CloudWatch Logs, from where users can view and analyze.

5.3. The Challenges of Logging

Among the challenges for logging with AWS Fargate, some of the most prevalent ones include:

1. Understanding log drivers: AWS Fargate supports two essential log drivers — awslogs and awsfirelens — each of which has its peculiar set up and log format. The process of comprehending these drivers can be complex, especially considering the various parameters they contain.

2. Restrictions with default log driver: The awslogs driver, although reliable, lacks the flexibility to forward logs to multiple destinations or transform logs. These restrictions can limit monitoring capabilities in certain scenarios.

3. Log retention: There is a default log retention period of 365 days in CloudWatch Logs, which may be unsuitable for some use cases. Changes to this retention period can be done, but they require additional manual configuration.

4. Costs: Logging can introduce additional costs as it works hand in hand with services like CloudWatch. Awareness of logging-related costs assists in managing budgets effectively.

5.4. Basics of Monitoring in AWS Fargate

Monitoring a containerized environment in AWS Fargate involves analyzing metrics and understanding the interactions between different components of the service. AWS provides monitoring metrics via CloudWatch, which offers numerable parameters for effective examination.

5.5. Monitoring Challenges

The challenges faced while performing monitoring tasks in AWS Fargate include:

1. Complexity: Monitoring in a serverless environment involves various services interacting. Understanding the relation between these services and identifying the cause of issues can be complex.

2. Granular data: By default, Fargate doesn't provide granular metrics down to the task level. To gain more details, the user must manually configure more in-depth metrics, which entails an understanding of CloudWatch insights.

3. Costs: Similar to logging, an increase in the detail and number of data points monitored escalates the overall costs incurred.

4. Limited out of the box insights: Fargate's out-of-the-box insights are limited and might not be adequate for advanced troubleshooting. Users may have to resort to custom metrics or third-party tools, which introduces additional complexity.

To optimally employ AWS Fargate, users must become proficient in conquering the hurdles that come with logging and monitoring systems. The complexities may initially seem daunting, but with clear apprehension of the underlying concepts and practical complexities, they can be navigated successfully. The investment in this understanding undoubtedly pays dividends when it comes to optimizing system performance or troubleshooting. The benefits hence, orbit around improved efficiency, cost-effectiveness, and overall system optimization.

Chapter 6. Evaluating Native AWS Solutions for Logging and Monitoring

As we delve into the subject, the influence of AWS' native solutions in logging and monitoring is paramount. AWS offers dedicated services for system analysis and oversight, namely AWS CloudWatch and CloudTrail, pertinent for optimizing system performance, identifying issues, and troubleshooting them within AWS Fargate.

6.1. AWS CloudWatch: A Detailed Look

AWS CloudWatch is a monitoring and observability service, equipped to offer valuable data and actionable insights to optimize applications, understand system-wide performance, and troubleshoot issues effectively.

CloudWatch can collect operational and performance data in the form of logs, metrics, and events, offering a unified platform to monitor your AWS resources, applications, and services running on AWS.

6.1.1. CloudWatch Logs

CloudWatch Logs is a feature within CloudWatch that allows you to monitor, store, and access your log files from Amazon Elastic Compute Cloud (Amazon EC2) instances, AWS CloudTrail, Route 53, and other sources. You can centralize the logs from all your systems, applications, and AWS services that you use, in one single, highly scalable service.

The power of CloudWatch Logs stems from two components:

Table 1. 1+ |

CloudWatch Logs Insights

This offers an interactive and controlled interface to explore, analyze, and visualize your logs. It is a fully integrated, extensible log analytics service, allowing you to derive actionable insights in seconds.

CloudWatch Logs Agent

This is a daemon that sends log data to the service from EC2 instances. It can even watch and forward custom log files.

6.1.2. CloudWatch Metrics

Alongside logs, CloudWatch also deals with metrics, which are fundamental data points for changes in resources. You can use metrics to calculate statistics, set alarms, or automate actions based on specific conditions. CloudWatch Metrics includes your custom AWS service metrics and application metrics, facilitating easier visibility into system-wide performance and operational health.

6.2. AWS CloudTrail: A Thorough Examination

AWS CloudTrail is a web service that records AWS API calls for your account and delivers log files to you. With CloudTrail, you gain increased visibility into your user and resource activity by recording AWS Management Console actions and AWS SDKs, command-line tools, and other AWS services.

If CloudWatch is the eyes of your monitoring efforts, CloudTrail could be deemed as the memory, as it records and stores the event history of your AWS account.

6.2.1. CloudTrail Log File Integrity Validation

An exceptional feature provided by AWS CloudTrail is log file integrity validation. This enables you to verify the integrity of log files and detect whether it's been tampered with or remained unchanged.

6.2.2. CloudTrail Insights

With CloudTrail Insights, you can identify unusual operational activity that may indicate unauthorized access or misused resources. It analyzes write management events for patterns that might signify that AWS resources are being misused, helping you to spot potential security threats.

6.3. Analyzing AWS CloudWatch and CloudTrail in the Context of AWS Fargate

These native tools can be leveraged for AWS Fargate but come with challenges. Although CloudWatch provides metrics for many AWS services, with AWS Fargate, you have limited visibility into your running containers. As for CloudTrail, while it provides visibility into the administrative actions taken on your Fargate clusters, it doesn't capture what is occurring within the containers.

6.4. Choosing the Right Tool for the Job

CloudWatch and CloudTrail provide extensive monitoring and logging solutions, but to fully evaluate their applicability to AWS Fargate, specific challenges concerning container visibility must be met. You need to tailor your approach to cater to container-specific monitoring and logging needs.

Despite minor limitations for users seeking a more detailed view into their running containers, both services have become indispensable for monitoring and logging CMS based on AWS Fargate. Implementing them necessitates a nuanced understanding of their functions, benefits, and downfalls in the context of specific Fargate-related challenges.

Chapter 7. Exploring Third-Party Tools for AWS Fargate Monitoring

One significant consideration when monitoring AWS Fargate is the use of third-party tools. These can provide different perspectives, additional metrics, or enhanced data handling capabilities that you might not get directly from AWS. Here, we'll look at some common third-party tools that can aid in our quest to master Fargate monitoring.

7.1. Datadog

Datadog is a popular monitoring service that provides full visibility into the performance of modern applications by integrating and automating infrastructure monitoring, application performance tracking, and log management.

When using Datadog with AWS Fargate, you can access metrics such as CPU and memory usage, plus Datadog's unique, additional metrics such as the number of tasks per service, the number of running tasks, and many more. This can give you a much more comprehensive view of your Fargate deployment.

Integration between Fargate and Datadog is seamless. As you launch your Fargate tasks or services, you can configure Datadog's Docker agent in your task definition. Here's how it would look in simple asciidoc style code:

```
containerDefinitions: [
  {
    name: "datadog-agent",
```

```
      image: "datadog/agent:latest",
      essential: true,
      // more configurations
    }
  ]
```

7.2. New Relic

Like Datadog, New Relic offers an integrated platform where you can
track your infrastructure, applications, errors, and logs all in one
place. Specifically for Fargate, you can collect, visualize, and alert on
your metrics similar to Datadog.

To add New Relic's monitoring capabilities to your Fargate
deployment, you need the New Relic infrastructure agent container
to run alongside your application's container. The task definition
should look similar to this:

```
containerDefinitions: [
  {
    name: "new-relic-infrastructure",
    image: "newrelic/infrastructure",
    essentials: true,
    // further configurations
  }
]
```

7.3. Splunk

Another capable tool in our arsenal is Splunk, which specializes in
analyzing and visualizing machine data. Splunk has an AWS-specific
solution that includes pre-built dashboards and analytics tailored for
various AWS services, including Fargate.

Splunk's Forwarder collects logs and metrics from Fargate containers and sends them to Splunk for monitoring and analysis. This Forwarder needs to be launched as a sidecar container alongside your application's container. Here's a simple example:

```
containerDefinitions: [
  {
    name: "splunk-forwarder",
    image: "splunk/splunk:latest",
    essential: true,
    // additional configurations
  }
]
```

Each of these solutions provides its own advantages in certain contexts, and your specific use case should guide the choice. The one common theme is that all these tools require a sidecar container running alongside the main application container, emphasizing the importance of robust containerization knowledge when working with Fargate.

7.4. Selecting the Right Tools for Monitoring

Choosing the right third-party tool can depend on a broad range of factors. Businesses must consider their specific needs, budget constraints, and existing tech stack while assessing potential monitoring solutions. Some of the key factors to consider while selecting monitoring tools are:

1. Compatibility: The tool should easily integrate with your AWS Fargate services.

2. Cost-Effective: While some tools offer extensive capabilities, they

often come at a higher cost. Balancing your requirements and budget is crucial.

3. Ease of Use: The tool should be user-friendly and offer intuitive interfaces for non-technical team members to understand and draw insights.

4. Real-Time Alerts: An efficient system should alert the team about critical events that may affect the system's performance, minimizing downtime.

5. Detailed Reporting: A good tool should provide extensive reporting capabilities for in-depth understanding.

Remember, each tool comes with its unique features and value proposition. Make sure it aligns with your overall operational goals and strategies. Ultimately, your technology choice should enhance productivity and not add complexities.

Let this exploration of third-party monitoring tools for AWS Fargate be a stepping stone towards your quest of mastering container orchestration. As with any technology, the key to success lies in understanding the intricacies of the tool and effectively applying it to derive meaningful insights that bring value to your operations.

Chapter 8. Best Practices for AWS Fargate Logging

Understanding the powerful capabilities of AWS Fargate in orchestrating container deployments comes with a profound appreciation of logging. Observability, a key concern in your modern cloud applications, takes a front seat when ensuring the smooth operation of software components. The rigorous demands of working in a microservices architecture necessitate strategies for optimal logging. With AWS Fargate, you don't just monitor your applications, but also dive deeper into problem analysis and solution.

8.1. Setting Up the Logs

AWS Fargate uses Amazon CloudWatch to store and monitor logs for your benefit. This integrated service supports a myriad of use-cases from auditing resource changes to tracking network-flow logs.

To begin, create a new task definition or update an existing one. Under the "Container Definitions" section, you'll find the "storage and logging" option. As you toggle the log configuration settings, you'll find parameters that indicate the Log driver, Options, and Secret Options. For AWS Fargate users, the Log driver will be 'awslogs'.

Under Options, specify the region (region), log group (awslogs-group), stream prefix (awslogs-stream-prefix), be sure to replace the elastic network interface (ENI) ID and, eventually, the log delivery status (awslogs-create-group).

Note that the Secret Options are not applicable unless you plan on using a different log driver that requires private information such as usernames or passwords.

8.2. Log Stream Management

Amazon CloudWatch operates by grouping log streams into log groups. Each group houses logs of a particular type or from a specific source. You have the option to define retention policies on your log groups that determine how long logs are kept before deletion.

The log stream prefix parameter is advisable to be descriptive of the source that's generating the logs. Post-deployment, you can use this prefix to filter out logs for each revision of your tasks.

By design, a new CloudWatch log stream is created for every new AWS Fargate task that is launched and gets assigned a unique log stream name, consisting of the stream-prefix parameter followed by the unique task and container instance IDs.

8.3. Parsing Logs

AWS Fargate logs are not automatically parsed to a structured format out of the box. Instead, Fargate uses JSON formatted logs which can be quite inconvenient at times due to the intimidating verbosity. Thankfully, AWS provides a way to parse these logs using an AWS Lambda function which is triggered whenever a new log stream is created in CloudWatch.

Through the defined Lambda function and a pattern-matching method, logs can be parsed and formatted into a more readable structure.

8.4. Troubleshooting with Logs

Troubleshooting with logs is a critical aspect of managing any application. AWS Fargate allows you to query your logs directly in CloudWatch Logs using CloudWatch Logs Insights.

CloudWatch Logs Insights includes a purpose-built query language with a few simple but powerful commands. This allows you to extract fields from JSON log events, filter logs by date ranges, and create visualizations of log data to better understand patterns, find anomalies, etc.

8.5. Centralized Logging

Cross-regional and cross-account log collection is a critical aspect of maintaining a secure and efficient logging strategy. By centralizing your logs through CloudWatch Logs, you can import logs from external systems or third-party providers and set up monitoring configurations across regions and accounts.

Helpful in creating a unified and organized view of all your data, centralized logging allows for better anomaly detection and faster incidence response.

8.6. The Bridge to Log Analytics Solutions

Regardless of the depth and monitoring capabilities of CloudWatch, you may already have a preferred, invested, third-party log analytics solution where AWS log ingestion is as easy as setting up suitable plugins or forwarders.

Services like Datadog, Splunk, and Sumo Logic are sought-after alternatives for their robust log aggregation, visualization, and analytics prowess that simplify the pathway from data to insights.

In conclusion, AWS Fargate logging is an essential component for application developers and system administrators striving to maintain high levels of system performance. With awslogs as the standard log driver, CloudWatch as the integrated service, and options to connect with third-party analytics services, AWS Fargate ensures that you are never short of insights. Ensuring you adhere to best practices will always keep you a step ahead in troubleshooting and optimizing your container applications.

Chapter 9. Optimizing Alert Management in AWS Fargate

Once we understand the intricacies of logging and monitoring with AWS Fargate, optimizing the alert management inevitably becomes the next big challenge. This involves refining the frequency, parameters, and recipients of the alert notifications not only to keep relevant teams informed but also to prevent them from being overwhelmed by the clutter of non-critical alerts.

9.1. Establishing Alert Policies

Setting up effective alert policies is the cornerstone to great management. With AWS Fargate, you can implement advanced alert policies in Container Insights. Alert policies in AWS Fargate allow you to set alarm thresholds for your container metrics.

1. From the AWS Management Console, navigate to CloudWatch, then Alarms.

2. Click on the "Create Alarm" button.

3. Select "Container Insights" as the alarm type and choose the container service for which you'd like to create the alarm.

4. Define the alert metrics and set your threshold.

5. Define the actions AWS should take when the threshold has been exceeded. This could be sending notifications to an SNS Topic or triggering Automation Workflows.

6. Lastly, review your setting and click on the "Create Alarm" button again to complete the process.

It is essential to strike a balance while defining the thresholds so that you aren't swamped with unnecessary alerts, yet nothing critical slips your notice.

9.2. Fine-tuning Alerts with AWS CloudWatch

AWS CloudWatch offers several fine-tuning options to create efficient and meaningful alerts. AWS Fargate integrates seamlessly with CloudWatch resulting in robust and highly customizable alert management.

You can fine-tune the timing of your alerts using the 'Period' field while setting the alarm. This allows you to control how long the threshold should be breached before an alert gets fired. For example, setting the 'Period' to 5 minutes will fire the alert only if the particular metric remains over the threshold for an entire 5 minutes.

In addition to 'Period', AWS CloudWatch provides 'Statistic' and 'Datapoints to Alarm' options. 'Statistic' provides the ability to alarm on average, maximum, minimum, and sample count, or percentile statistics over the defined 'Period'. Using the 'Datapoints to Alarm' field, you can define the number of evaluation periods for which the alarm state should breach the threshold before firing an alert.

Effective utilization of these fields and testing the fine-tuned alerts over a period ensures an optimized alert mechanism, thus focusing on necessary alerts and avoiding alert fatigue.

9.3. Integrating with Notification Channels

Post defining alerts, ensuring they reach the right audience at the right time is pivotal. AWS Fargate streamlines this via Amazon Simple Notification Service (SNS) and Simple Email Service (SES).

You can define SNS topics while creating alerts and CloudWatch will send alert notifications to the corresponding subscribers. AWS supports a variety of subscription types such as email, SMS, HTTP, SQS, Lambda, and even mobile push notifications.

For email alerts, you can use the SES. It is a scalable and cost-effective email service suitable for marketing, notification, or transactional emails. Coupled with CloudWatch and SNS, AWS Fargate ensures that the alerts are sent as swiftly as possible to relevant recipients.

9.4. Alert Management with Third-party Tools

While AWS native tools offer substantial alert management capabilities, third-party tools such as Datadog, NewRelic, and Splunk can further amplify the alerting and incident response capabilities.

These tools provide features such as machine learning-based alert tuning, alert grouping, multi-channel notifications, incident management, and automated response workflows. They work nicely with AWS Fargate through plugins, AWS API, and by fetching logs and metrics from different AWS services, providing you with an extra layer of sophistication and efficiency.

9.5. Conclusion: Enhancing Alert Management Effectiveness

Optimized alert management with AWS Fargate ultimately boils down to three crucial factors: defining meaningful alert policies, alert fine-tuning using AWS CloudWatch, and effective delivery of alert notifications via SNS and SES. It's also wise to consider third-party tools for additional features and escalated capabilities when needed.

The journey to optimizing your alert-management strategy involves periods of testing, adjustment, and learning. With careful consideration of your unique use-case and diligent execution of the strategies outlined above, you can significantly enhance your system performance, troubleshooting, and overall operational efficiency.

Chapter 10. Building Resilient Systems: Troubleshooting and Debugging in AWS Fargate

AWS Fargate's inherent merit is its ability to allow developers to focus on the application logic, leaving infrastructure maintenance tasks to AWS. However, when issues arise, Fargate's level of abstraction can make debugging and troubleshooting layers more challenging. This part of the report will discuss deep-dive approaches for effective troubleshooting and debugging in AWS Fargate.

10.1. Understanding AWS Fargate's Operational Overheads

Before diving into specific problem-solving methods, it's essential to comprehend the operational overheads that AWS Fargate presents. Every infrastructure has its own set of complexities and limitations, and understanding them is a precondition for efficient troubleshooting.

Your container tasks in Fargate run in a VPC, allocated with ENI (Elastic Network Interface), and are load balanced for effectively distributing the incoming traffic. While this setup ensures a robust, secure, and scalable environment for container tasks, the associated overhead may impact the operational observability. For instance, the ENI's IP address mapping can become complex in containers, affecting the forwarding of logs and metrics.

10.2. Logging in AWS Fargate

Logs are the primary source of truth when it comes to understanding a system's behavior. However, monitoring logs with AWS Fargate can be overwhelming, given the volume and complexity involved. Fortunately, AWS provides CloudWatch Logs, a service that allows you to monitor, store, and access your log files from Amazon EC2 instances.

Start by enabling the awslogs driver in your task definition, which defaults to sending logs to CloudWatch Logs group in the format /aws/ecs/{task-definition-family}. However, the volume of log data can get quite high, and CloudWatch pricing is based on total log data sent to the service. It's often a delicate balancing act between the level of logging verbosity and associated costs. Consider adjusting your application's logging levels to include error-level messages primarily, excluding debug and info logs based on your application's needs.

10.3. Monitoring Container Health and Performance

Understanding AWS Fargate's performance is a crucial part of managing the service. AWS provides CloudWatch, a built-in service for monitoring resources run on AWS.

In order to get started with CloudWatch, you should first ensure that your task definition includes the necessary parameters for sending metrics. In the ECS task definition JSON, set "requiresCompatibilities" to include "FARGATE" and specify a supported CPU and memory value under "cpu" and "memory".

For each AWS Fargate task, watch out for metrics like CPU and memory utilization, network bytes and packets. Recognizing abnormal patterns in these metrics will help you identify impending issues and proactively troubleshoot them. Besides, AWS CloudWatch Alarms can notify you of potential problems if a metric exceeds a specified threshold over a determined number of periods.

10.4. Debugging AWS Fargate Container

Debugging containers in AWS Fargate requires a well-planned approach due to the lack of direct access to the Fargate infrastructure. Further, it mandates an understanding of the lifecycle of a Fargate Task, the associated states, and when a task transitions from one state to another.

You can use the `DescribeTasks` API call to obtain metadata about your running tasks. It shows task-level data along with data for all the containers running within it. For further introspection, another powerful tool at your disposal is the `aws ecs execute-command`. Here, system and debugging tools installed in the container become significantly helpful.

One important consideration while debugging containers is interception of outbound connections. In Fargate, tasks are assigned their own IP addresses. Therefore, understanding the transaction of packets within the VPC becomes important for intercepting traffic in a containerized environment.

10.5. Implementing Alerting Mechanism

Time matters immensely during debugging. An effective alerting system can not only help you react rapidly to issues but can also provide the root cause analysis that accelerates the debugging process.

Look out for common errors like Connection Timeouts, HTTP Server Errors, and Insufficient CPU Configurations. Using Amazon CloudWatch Events, you can set up alerts for abnormal changes in these metrics. Implement automation wherever possible to receive alerts when an ECS Task State changes or when ECS drains connections from a container instance.

To sum up, building resilient systems with AWS Fargate begins with a robust plan for logging, monitoring, and debugging. A well-planned observability stack, coupled with a deep understanding of Fargate's operational overheads, can go a long way in ensuring the resilience of your tasks running in AWS Fargate. Remember, systems aren't resilient by accident — they are consciously made to be so.

Chapter 11. Conclusion and Future Trends in AWS Fargate Logging and Monitoring

In viewing the entirety of our exploration on AWS Fargate's logging and monitoring landscape, it's indisputably clear that while technologies have progressed considerably to aid in simplifying container management, complexities and challenges remain. Amazon Web Services (AWS) Fargate in particular, despite being an excellent tool for running containers without managing servers or clusters, has shown a potential to occasionally perplex users with its logging and monitoring intricacies.

11.1. The Summary Recall

To recap, we explored the fundamental concept of using AWS Fargate for efficient container management, detailing how to deploy applications via Fargate tasks, discussed the role of task definitions, and explored how AWS's other services like Amazon CloudWatch and AWS X-Ray are instrumental in Fargate's logging and monitoring.

We also covered common obstacles we face when working with Fargate, primarily revolving around log collection, issues of visibility into running tasks, and the challenges related to cost management and resource allocation. Strategies for troubleshooting and mitigation of these challenges were the core focus, namely tools and practices such as container insights, log streams, and Fargate Spot to manage costs.

11.2. Anticipating Future Trends

As technology and computing evolve, so too will AWS Fargate. To stay ahead, it's critical to be cognizant of emerging trends and developments such as the growing use of microservices architecture, enhanced automation, and the increased focus on security.

Cloud-based services have broadened the usage of microservices architecture. This method of developing applications is no longer a trend, but an indispensable part of software development today. Fargate fits seamlessly into this paradigm, enabling teams to manage containers and deploy microservices without the need to manage the underlying infrastructure. As the adoption of microservices grows, we can foresee an increased utilization of Fargate.

Automation is undeniable in its capacity not only to improve operational efficiency but also to reduce error rates dramatically. We anticipate seeing more smart automations offered by Fargate. This could involve intelligent scaling in response to traffic patterns, optimizing resource allocation, or automated logging and monitoring based on user-defined thresholds and metrics.

Finally, security considerations are of the utmost importance. As cyber threats continue to evolve and increase in sophistication, maintaining a secure container environment like Fargate is going to be paramount. Users can expect AWS to continually enhance security measures and provide additional tools for monitoring and mitigating potential threats.

11.3. The Bottom Line

The key to maximizing AWS Fargate's potential and turning challenges into assets lies in a deep understanding of its underlying mechanisms, common obstacles, and the ability to leverage its integrated AWS services effectively. Continuous learning, keeping up with AWS updates, and adopting the best practices for container management will be invaluable.

The nature of AWS Fargate's logging and monitoring complexities also underscores the importance of developing competent troubleshooting skills. Learning to navigate logs effectively, understanding metrics and their interpretation, grasping the convolution of resource allocation and cost management - these are the technical proficiencies that will make all the difference.

As we move into the future, it's clear that AWS Fargate will continue to play a key role in managing and deploying containers. Regardless of the challenges, the advantages of a serverless, fully managed container service are too compelling to overlook. A future where we see more relaxed plugin requirements, deeper integrations with other AWS services, improved automation, and a more fortified security framework, is not too far off.

So, as we close out this exhaustive look at AWS Fargate's logging and monitoring landscape, it's worth acknowledging the journey we've undertaken to understand, contextualize, and anticipate the changes in this rapidly advancing field. It's been a winding road, but one that is gradually giving way to clarity and understanding.

Stay ahead of the curve. Embrace the complex, and most importantly, never stop learning. That, in essence, is the key to successful navigation in the ocean of AWS Fargate's logging and monitoring.

www.ingramcontent.com/pod-product-compliance
Lightning Source LLC
Chambersburg PA
CBHW071046260726
48661CB00007B/3171